NEW ENGLAND PATRIOTS

BY BARRY WILNER

The Child's World®

Published by The Child's World®
1980 Lookout Drive • Mankato, MN 56003-1705
800-599-READ • www.childsworld.com

Acknowledgments
The Child's World®: Mary Berendes, Publishing Director
Red Line Editorial: Editorial direction
The Design Lab: Design
Amnet: Production

Design Element: Dean Bertoncelj/Shutterstock Images
Photographs ©: Steven Senne/AP Images, cover; Elise
Amendola/AP Images, 5; Damian Strohmeyer/AP
Images, 7; AP Images, 9; Charles Krupa/AP Images, 11;
Richard Cavalleri/Shutterstock Images, 13; Michael
Dwyer/AP Images, 14-15; Jeff Lewis/Icon SMI/Newscom,
17; Ben Liebenberg/AP Images, 19; Joseph Sohm Visions
of America/Newscom, 21; Ray Stubblebine/AP Images,
23; Winslow Townson/AP Images, 25; Aaron M. Sprecher/
AP Images, 27; Phelan M. Ebenhack/AP Images, 29

ISBN 9781631439896
LCCN 2014959659

Printed in the United States of America
Mankato, MN
July, 2015
PA02265

ABOUT THE AUTHOR

Barry Wilner has written more than 40 books, including many for young readers. He is a sports writer for the Associated Press and has covered such events as the Super Bowl, Olympics, and World Cup. He lives in Garnerville, New York.

TABLE OF CONTENTS

GO, PATRIOTS!

The Patriots started playing in 1960. The team has had many good seasons. But in recent years, they have been almost unstoppable. They won more games than any other team from 2000 to 2014. And from 2003 to 2008, they won 82 out of 100 games. That's the best 100-game stretch in league history. Let's meet the New England Patriots.

Patriots wide receiver Julian Edelman sprints for a touchdown in a game against the Denver Broncos on November 2, 2014.

WHO ARE THE PATRIOTS?

The New England Patriots are one of the 32 teams in the National Football League (NFL). The NFL includes the American Football Conference (AFC) and the National Football Conference (NFC). The winner of the AFC plays the winner of the NFC in the **Super Bowl**. The Patriots play in the East Division of the AFC. They won the Super Bowl after the 2001, 2003, 2004, and 2014 seasons.

Quarterback Tom Brady (12) leads the team onto the field before a game against the Miami Dolphins on October 27, 2013.

WHERE THEY CAME FROM

During the Patriots' first 11 years, the team played in four stadiums around Massachusetts. In 1971, they finally settled in Foxborough. They changed their name from Boston to New England to reflect where their fans came from. Patriots fans often come from the New England states of Massachusetts, Maine, Rhode Island, Vermont, New Hampshire, and Connecticut.

Running back Jim Nance (35) squeezes between defenders for a touchdown on November 15, 1970. Nance is in the Patriots Hall of Fame.

WHO THEY PLAY

The Patriots play 16 games each season. With so few games, each one is important. Every year, the Patriots play two games against each of the other three teams in their division: the Buffalo Bills, the Miami Dolphins, and the New York Jets. The Patriots and the Jets are big **rivals**. Fans from Boston and New York always like their teams to beat each other. The cities are close together. Many fans drive to the other team's stadium to see their team play.

Tight end Rob Gronkowski breaks away from a tackle in a game against the rival New York Jets on October 16, 2014.

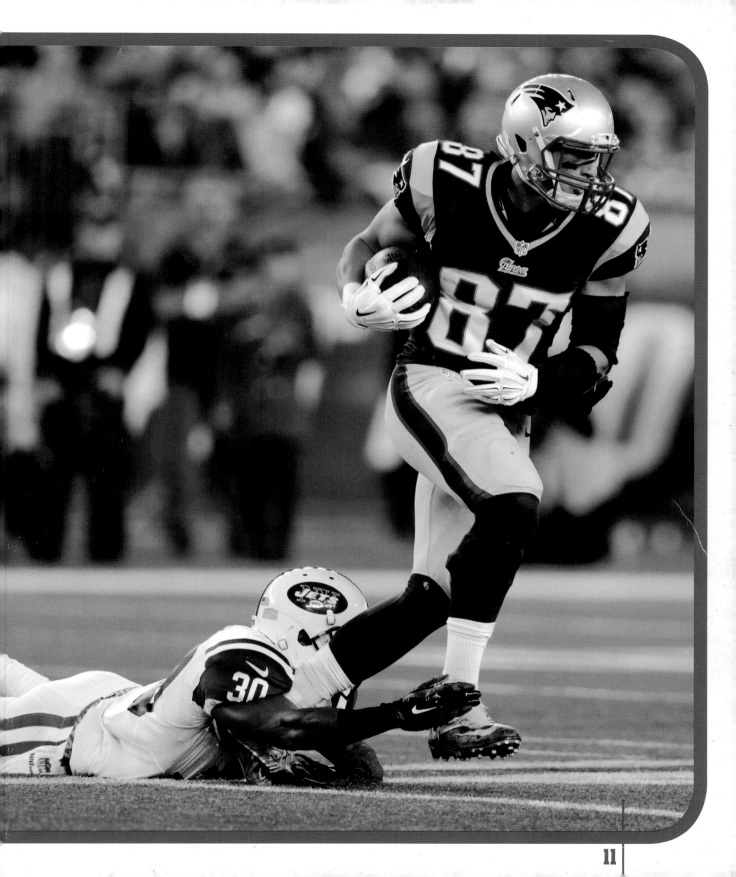

WHERE THEY PLAY

illette Stadium has been the Patriots' home since 2002. It seats nearly 69,000 people. The stadium was built next to Foxboro Stadium, where the Patriots played until 2001. Today, a shopping mall called Patriot Place is next to the stadium. The Patriots Hall of Fame is part of the mall. Gillette Stadium has a lighthouse and bridge by one entrance. They represent the New England region. The lighthouse sends light high into the sky during night games.

Gillette Stadium is located between Boston, Massachusetts, and Providence, Rhode Island.

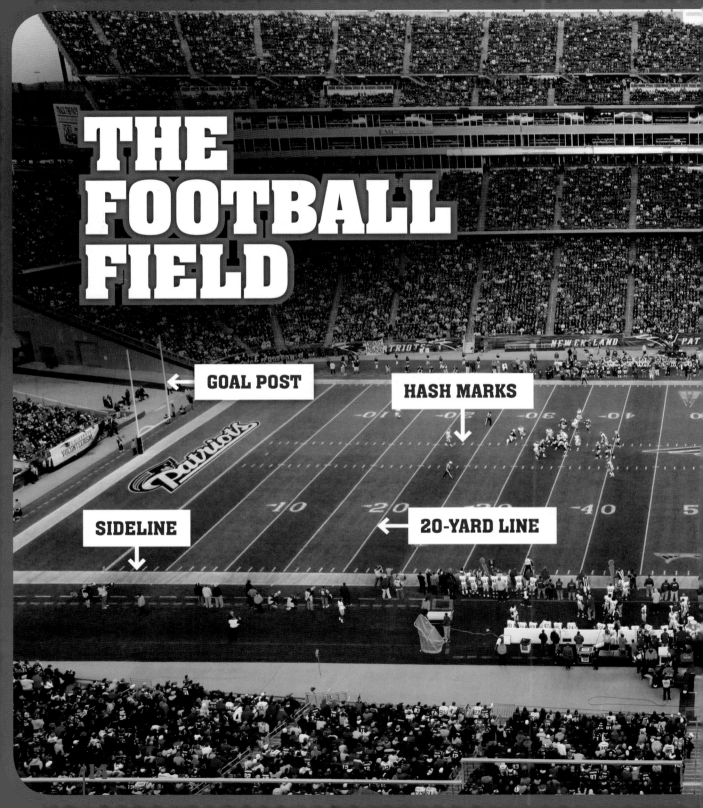

THE FOOTBALL FIELD

GOAL POST

HASH MARKS

SIDELINE

20-YARD LINE

BENCH AREA

END ZONE

MIDFIELD

END LINE

GOAL LINE

40 30 20 10

40- 30- 20- 10-

BIG DAYS

The Patriots have had some great moments in their history. Here are three of the greatest:

2004—The Patriots won their third Super Bowl in four years. Safety Rodney Harrison **intercepted** a pass with nine seconds left in the Super Bowl on February 6, 2005. The Patriots beat the Philadelphia Eagles 24-21.

2007—The Patriots went an amazing 16-0 during the regular season. Tom Brady threw 50 **touchdown** passes. Randy Moss set a record with 23 touchdown catches.

Rodney Harrison (37) runs down the field after his second interception of the day on February 6, 2005.

2014—Tom Brady led the Patriots to their eighth Super Bowl appearance. The team faced off against the Seattle Seahawks on February 1, 2015. Safety Malcolm Butler intercepted a pass at the goal line with 23 seconds left to seal a 28-24 win.

TOUGH DAYS

ootball is a hard game. Even the best teams have rough games and seasons. Here are some of the toughest times in Patriots history:

1970—The Boston Patriots' last season was awful. They went 2-12, worse than every other team. They scored only 149 points.

1990—The Patriots were the NFL's worst team again under new coach Rod Rust. They went 1-15 and lost their last 14 games.

2008—The 2007 Patriots' chance for a perfect season ended with a 17-14 loss to the New York Giants in the

The Giants scored with 35 seconds left to end the Patriots' perfect season on February 3, 2008.

Super Bowl on February 3, 2008. The Giants scored the winning touchdown with 35 seconds left in the game.

MEET THE FANS

It gets very cold in New England late in the season. Still, Patriots fans always show up at the stadium. The team sells out all of its home games. People come from across the country to see the Patriots play. Many fans come early to **tailgate** or shop at Patriot Place before **kickoff**. Patriots fans have enjoyed many exciting moments. But win or lose, they always support their team.

New England Patriots fans show their support for their team.

HEROES THEN

In the 1960s, the Patriots' best players were Gino Cappelletti and Nick Buoniconti. Cappelletti was a great receiver and team leader. He also played defensive back and kicker. Buoniconti spent seven seasons as a middle linebacker for the Patriots. He was an outstanding tackler. Like Buoniconti, Andre Tippett was a hard-hitting linebacker for New England. He would often **sack** the other team's quarterback. Tippett and Buoniconti are in the Pro Football Hall of Fame. Guard John Hannah is, too. He played 13 seasons for the Patriots and started all 183 games he appeared in. Hannah was considered one of the best blockers in history.

Linebacker Andre Tippett slams Jets quarterback Ken O'Brien to the ground on December 28, 1985. Tippett has the most sacks in team history.

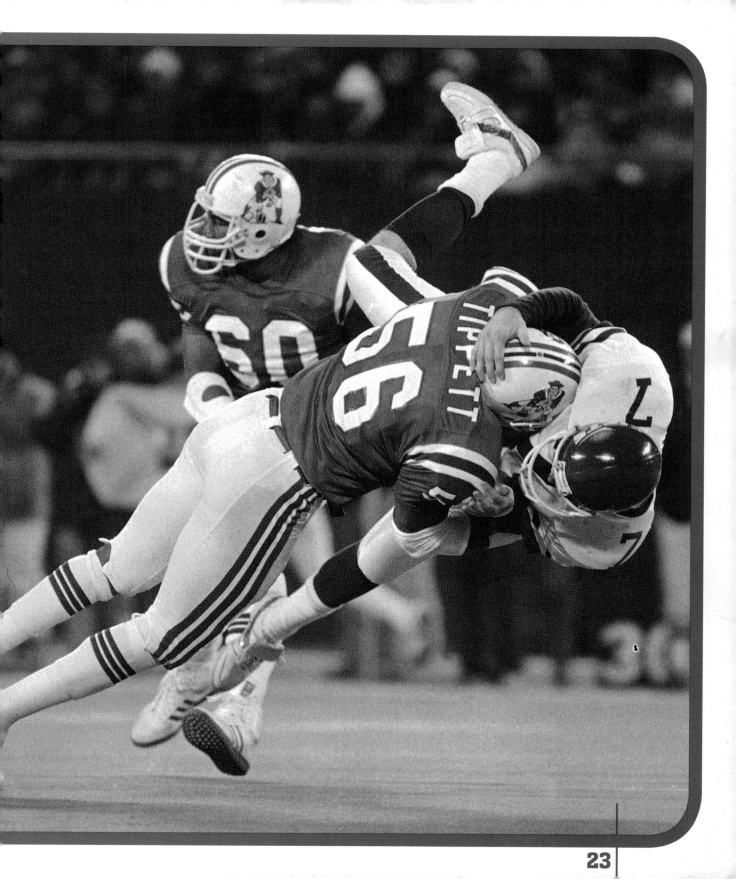

HEROES NOW

Tom Brady was not chosen until the sixth round of the 2000 **NFL Draft**. But he has become one of the greatest quarterbacks in NFL history. "Tom Terrific" became the starter in 2001. He has won four Super Bowls as the starting quarterback. This is tied for the most ever. Tight end Rob Gronkowski is one of Brady's favorite targets. Other teams usually need two players to cover him. He caught a league-high 17 touchdown passes in 2011. Stephen Gostkowski is one the best kickers in the NFL. He led the league in scoring during the 2012, 2013, and 2014 seasons.

Tom Brady signals a play from the line of scrimmage. Tom Brady has led the Patriots to six Super Bowls. No other quarterback has made it to six.

GEARING UP

NFL players wear team uniforms. They wear helmets and pads to keep them safe. Cleats help them make quick moves and run fast. Some players wear extra gear for protection.

THE FOOTBALL

NFL footballs are made of leather. Under the leather is a lining that fills with air to give the ball its shape. The leather has bumps, or "pebbles." These help players grip the ball. Laces help players control their throws. Footballs are also called "pigskins" because some of the first balls were made from pig bladders. Today they are made of leather from cows.

Some players wear braces on their arms or legs for extra protection.

HELMET

SHOULDER PADS

GLOVES

THIGH PADS

FOOTBALL

CLEATS

SPORTS STATS

Here are some of the all-time career records for the New England Patriots. All the stats are through the 2014 season.

PASSING YARDS	
Tom Brady	53,258
Drew Bledsoe	29,657

RUSHING YARDS	
Sam Cunningham	5,453
Jim Nance	5,323

TOTAL TOUCHDOWNS	
Stanley Morgan	68
Rob Gronkowski	55

INTERCEPTIONS	
Ty Law	36
Raymond Clayborn	36

SACKS	
Andre Tippett	100
Willie McGinest	78

POINTS	
Stephen Gostkowski	1,179
Adam Vinatieri	1,158

Wide receiver Wes Welker caught 123 passes for the Patriots in 2009. It is the third-most receptions in a season in NFL history.

RECEPTIONS

Wes Welker 672

Troy Brown 557

GLOSSARY

intercepted when a player on the defense catches a forward pass

kickoff when one teams kicks the ball to the other to begin a game or series of plays

NFL Draft a meeting of all the NFL teams at which they choose college players to join them

rivals teams whose games bring out the greatest emotion between the players and the fans on both sides

sack when the quarterback is tackled behind the line of scrimmage before he can throw the ball

Super Bowl the championship game of the NFL, played between the winner of the AFC and the NFC

tailgate when fans gather outside of the stadium before a game to picnic around their vehicles

touchdown play in which the ball is held in the other team's end zone, resulting in six points

FIND OUT MORE

IN THE LIBRARY

Glaser, Jason. *Today's Sports Greats: Tom Brady*.
New York: Gareth Stevens, 2011.

Glennon, Sean. *Tom Brady vs. the NFL*. Chicago:
Triumph Books, 2012.

Price, Christopher. *New England Patriots: The Complete
Illustrated History*. Minneapolis: MVP Books, 2013.

ON THE WEB

Visit our Web site for links about the New England Patriots:
childsworld.com/links

*Note to Parents, Teachers, and Librarians: We routinely verify our Web links to make
sure they are safe and active sites. So encourage your readers to check them out!*

INDEX